THE OFFICIAL

Freebies®

for
Teachers

**Something
for Nothing
or Next to
Nothing!**

By the Editors of *FREEBIES* Magazine

Illustrated by Jim Auckland

LOWELL HOUSE JUVENILE

LOS ANGELES

CONTEMPORARY BOOKS

CHICAGO

Acknowledgments

It is difficult to put together a book of this nature without the help of talented and dedicated people working together. The staff at **FREEBIES** has a special thanks for the commitment of Lowell House to this project. Their support made it happen.

Special mention must be given to Joanna Siebert, Shellie Pomeroy, and the rest of the crew at Lowell House for the editing, the design, and the final push to complete this project.

A thank-you is also reserved for Brandy Marcum for her help and guidance. And a very special thank-you goes to Amy Richter. She provided the extra spark and energy needed in the research and coordination of the material in this book.

Lowell House books can be purchased at special discounts when ordered in bulk for premiums and special sales. Contact Department TC at the following address:

Lowell House Juvenile
2020 Avenue of the Stars, Suite 300
Los Angeles, CA 90067

ISBN: 1-56565-914-7

Library of Congress Catalog Card Number: 94-664208

Manufactured in the United States of America

10 9 8 7 6 5 4 3 2

Contents

Introduction

About This Book

Freebies for Teachers contains some great freebie offers that are sure to appeal to teachers and students alike, but you don't have to be a teacher to order from this book. Each offer has been described as accurately as possible to help you decide which offers are best for you.

Unlike offers in other "get things free" books, we have confirmed that each supplier wants you to have the offers listed in this book, and each supplier has agreed to have adequate stock on hand to honor all properly made requests. Many suppliers will make quantity discounts available. If you see something you like, write and ask about quantity discounts.

Some teachers have written and told us that they use the offers to set up a writing lesson. Students look through ***Freebies for Teachers*** and select an offer (be aware that some of the offers are not appropriate for children). The letter writing encourages good penmanship and spelling and teaches kids the proper way to write a business-type letter.

How to Use *Freebies for Teachers*

1. **Follow the directions.** Each offer specifies how to order the freebie. Some offers may ask for an LSASE (a long envelope with your name and complete mailing address with first-class postage affixed). Be sure to check the amount of postage requested; some offers may require two first-class stamps. Also, offers from Canada will require extra postage. Since postal rates can change, check with your local post office to determine the correct first-class postage to Canada. If a small postage-and-handling (P&H) fee is requested, include the proper amount (a check or money order is usually preferred). Some suppliers

may wait for out-of-town checks to clear before honoring requests. Do not send coins. Coins add weight, which requires extra postage, and can jam postal machinery.

2. **Print all information.** Not everyone's handwriting is easy to read. On your request, neatly print your name, address, the complete spelling of your city, and the correct abbreviation of your state. Be sure to include your return address on the outside of your mailing envelope. Be specific: indicate desired quantities and color preferences if the offer allows such choices.

3. **Allow time for your request to be processed and sent.** Some suppliers send their offers by first-class mail. Others use bulk-rate mail, which can take up to eight weeks. Suppliers get thousands of requests each year and may process them slowly or right away, depending on the time of year.

4. **What to do if you are unhappy with your freebie product.** If you are unhappy or have complaints about an offer, or if you have not received an offer within eight to ten weeks of your request, let ***FREEBIES*** know. Although the ***FREEBIES*** editors do not stock items or offer refunds, they can follow up on your complaints with any supplier. Suppliers that generate complaints will not be included in future editions. When writing a complaint, include the title of the book, the offer that you ordered, and the supplier's address. Send your complaints, comments, or suggestions to:

> ***FREEBIES for Teachers*** Book Editors
> 1135 Eugenia Place
> P.O. Box 5025
> Carpinteria, CA 93014-5025

5. **And there is more!** If you like the freebie offers in this book and want to see more free offers, then you should subscribe to ***FREEBIES*** Magazine. Five times a year, ***FREEBIES*** sends you a great magazine with approximately 100 current freebie offers in each issue. Purchasers of ***Freebies for Teachers*** can get a special price on a one-year/five-issue subscription of only $4.95. (The regular subscription rate is $8.95—you'll save $4.00. See the special offer on page 38.)

For the Classroom

A Dilly of a Plan

Lesson Plan

Where does food come from? **"A Marketing Dill-emma" is a FREE comprehensive lesson plan** designed to teach students where food comes from by following the "life" of a pickle from the cucumber patch to the grocery store shelf. The fun and entertaining kit is designed for the third and fourth grades; however, it can be adapted for use at any elementary grade level.

The kit includes everything you need to create a lively classroom discussion on food production, distribution, and consumption. You'll find activity sheets, a guide for individual student assignments and interactive classroom projects, a full-color poster, and plenty of background information for teachers. The unit even comes with a packet of cucumber seeds! Plus, you will receive a 3.9-foot-long blow-up pickle character for the classroom.

Send: Request on official school letterhead

Ask For: Pickle Lesson Plan

Mail To: Pickle Lesson Plan
P.O. Box 767 FB
Holmdel, NJ 07733

Limit: One per teacher

Math Activities
....
Math Booklet

Presented by Texas Instruments, this **free math booklet, "Uncovering Math with Your Family,"** contains fun activities for your students. Send this booklet home with kids who need extra practice or want to learn more math on their own. Written by leading educators, these activities nurture a child's natural curiosity. The booklet has four themes: Math in Your Home, Math on the Go, Math in Your Neighborhood, and Math in the Store.

Send: Your name & address
Ask For: "Uncovering Math with Your Family"
Mail To: M/S 3908 Freebie Offer
Family Math Booklet
Texas Instruments
P.O. Box 650311
Dallas, TX 75265-9862

History Lesson
....
Parchment Posters

Help your students understand the birth of the United States of America. Incorporate these **Colonial history parchment posters** into a lecture or use them in a creative bulletin board display for Presidents' Day, Memorial Day, Flag Day, or any day. Select either George Washington's Call to Arms or a pictorial history of the American flag. Each parchment paper reproduction is 14" x 16" and has an authentically aged look.

Send: $1.75 P&H for one; $2.75 for two
Ask For: Parchment (specify Call and/or Flag)
Mail To: S & H Trading Co.
1187 Coast Village Rd., #208
Montecito, CA 93108-2794

Beary Educational

Educator Kit

It's important for kids to learn at an early age about the food groups and eating right. With this **educator's kit,** you can teach your students about the food pyramid. The kit includes a storybook, informational leaflets, and a colorful poster to hang in the classroom. This kit is recommended for grades K–8.

Send: $1.00 P&H

Ask For: Educator Kit

Mail To: Oregon Washington California Pear Bureau
Studio FR-ED
4382 SE International Way
Milwaukie, OR 97222

Sight-Seeing Trip

Game Book

Have you ever wished you could take your students on a trip to the Smithsonian, a walk through Times Square, or a journey within the great state of Texas? Now you can "visit" one of these destinations with a **"Yes & Know Invisible Ink Quiz and Game Book."** You will receive one book (supplier's choice) featuring trivia, facts, fun games, and activities about Washington, DC, New York City, or Texas. Each 48-page book comes with a special highlighter pen used to reveal answers to the dozens of questions printed in invisible ink. These 5½" x 6" booklets are perfect as prizes or for classroom learning games.

Send: $2.00 P&H

Ask For: Invisible Ink Book (States)

Mail To: Alvin Peters Co., Dept. IVB
P.O. Box 2400, ESP
Albany, NY 12220-0400

Math Help
Computer Programs

Do you need a little help for your math students? Take advantage of this great offer and get **three math tutorial computer programs**. The programs are geared toward high school students who need to improve their skills in algebra, pre-calculus, and statistics. The programs come on a single 3½" disk for DOS-running IBM/compatibles (can also be run with Windows). You will also receive the 16-page *Laugh with Math* comic book and a **"Catalog for Mathephobics,"** which offers more learning tools.

Send:	$2.00 P&H
Ask For:	Math Tutorial Disk & *Laugh with Math*
Mail To:	Professor Weissman's Software
	246 Crafton Ave., Dept. FB
	Staten Island, NY 10314

Learning the Game of Politics
Dice Games

Make politics entertaining for your students using these vintage **original circa 1960 "Put and Take" dice games**. These games feature dice imprinted with the images of each major political party's mascot. This set makes a wonderful addition to the classroom games area and can be a fun way to learn about political parties and voting.

Send:	$2.00 P&H
Ask For:	Political Games
Mail To:	Joan Nykorchuk
	P.O. Box 47516
	Phoenix, AZ 85068-7516

Stuck in a Good Book!
Book Stickers

Inspire your students to read by rewarding them with one of these **200 happy book stickers**. Each of the stickers features a book with its own smiley face. These ½" colorful stickers come in a variety of bright designs. Kids love stickers, and these will make reading more fun.

Send: $1.00 P&H
Ask For: Happy Book Stickers
Mail To: The Very Best
P.O. Box 2838, Dept. F98
Long Beach, CA 90801-2838

Learning the ABC's
Flash Cards

Help young students learn their ABC's with these fun and colorful **ABC flash cards**. Each flash card has a letter of the alphabet along with a familiar word and picture. Children will love the creative drawings, and you will enjoy this approach to interactive learning.

Send: $1.00 P&H
Ask For: Flash Cards
Mail To: Flash Cards
P.O. Box 1-F
Stony Point, NY 10980

Get Set for School

School Supply Set

Get your pupils ready for class with this **cool school set**. The set consists of a colorfully designed pencil case, 6″ ruler, pencil and sharpener, and a dozen erasers. The scented erasers are shaped like fruits, flowers, and other sweet-smelling novelties. This set makes a terrific prize or gift for a special student on the first day of class!

Send: $2.00 P&H

Ask For: School Kit

Mail To: Jaye Products, Inc., Dept. 37
P.O. Box 10726
Naples, FL 34101

Bookplate Special

Book Labels

Make your mark in your classroom. You can neatly identify your favorite books with this **set of 10 art bookplates**. Each of these 2¾″ x 3¾″ gummed labels features a color art print. Stick them in textbooks or reading books so that everyone knows they belong in your classroom.

Send: $1.50 P&H

Ask For: 10 Bookplates

Mail To: Joan Nykorchuk
P.O. Box 47516
Phoenix, AZ 85068-7516

Healthy Attitude
Sticker Kit

This **FREE Grafeeties® sticker and catalog of 13 health and fitness messages** will help those health lessons "stick" with your students. Made of a unique elasticized foam, Grafeeties stickers have incredible sticking power but are still removable. Perfect for backpacks and in-line skates!

Send: $1.00 P&H
Ask For: Grafeeties Sticker and Catalog
Mail To: Grafeeties & Co.
1730 Blake St., #400
Denver, CO 80202

Un-Ruley!
Rolling Ruler

You will be amazed at what you can do with this ruler. From making basic lines to drawing perfect circles, this ruler can be used for many different classroom tasks. This multipurpose **rolling ruler** is actually six instruments in one: horizontal ruler, parallel ruler, compass, protractor, vertical ruler, and T square.

Send: $2.00 P&H
Ask For: Rolling Ruler
Mail To: Rolling Ruler
P.O. Box 411-F
Thiells, NY 10984

Fun with Phonics

Phonics Leaflet

Find out more about phonics with these **FREE "Tips on Helping Your Child to Read."** Written by a parent and former educator, this six-panel leaflet explains the concept of phonics, outlines basic teaching techniques, and advises parents on how to help their kids learn to read. This is a great tool to send home with your students so they can work on their reading skills with a parent.

Send: LSASE

Ask For: "Tips on Helping Your Child to Read"

Mail To: Learning Pyramid
P.O. Box 423411
Kissimmee, FL 34742-3411

Great American Heroes

Historical Booklet

Thomas Jefferson, Eleanor Roosevelt, and Martin Luther King, Jr., are just a few people whose ideas have influenced America as a nation. **"America's Heroes and You"** is a 25-page teaching booklet designed to inspire elementary and junior high school students by identifying qualities in heroes that kids can develop in themselves. It describes the lives of 11 famous Americans and includes discussion questions and activities.

Send: $2.00 P&H

Ask For: "America's Heroes and You"

Mail To: America's Heroes Offer
P.O. Box 161167
San Diego, CA 92176

Advice for the Gifted

Resources for Gifted Children

Teaching an intellectually gifted child can be a special challenge. To help you and your students take full advantage of the educational opportunities available, the National Association for Gifted Children is offering a **FREE "State Resource Sheet."** This directory of schools, organizations, and groups for gifted children is a wonderful reference guide. You will also receive a list of educational and fun Internet sites appropriate for kids.

> **Send:** LSASE
>
> **Ask For:** "State Resources" (specify your state) & "Safe Internet Sites"
>
> **Mail To:** NAGC
> 1707 L St. NW, Ste. 550
> Washington, DC 20036

Make Your Students Smile

Balloons

Looking for something cheerful to decorate your classroom with? Nothing brightens up a room like a balloon. With this offer you will receive **two 11" latex balloons**. The first balloon is bright yellow with a large smiley face. The second balloon is randomly chosen from an assortment of fun characters and designs. As a bonus, you will also receive at least two 9" latex balloons in fun colors. These high-quality latex balloons can be filled with helium or oxygen.

> **Send:** LSASE and 50¢ P&H
>
> **Ask For:** Smiley Face Balloon offer
>
> **Mail To:** Kristy's Balloons
> P.O. Box 234
> Stanton, MO 63079

Food for Thought
Brochure/Poster

Teach your students the importance of vitamins with this educational offer. **"Team Antioxidant: Because Your Body Is a Battleground,"** a fun and colorful brochure, provides essential nutrition tips and facts presented by "Team Antioxidant," a group of friendly vitamin characters. This piece explains how antioxidants in the body protect against free radicals and chronic diseases such as cancer and heart disease. The brochure opens into a poster to hang in your classroom.

Send:	$2.00 P&H
Ask For:	"Team Antioxidant: Because Your Body Is a Battleground"
Mail To:	"Team Antioxidant: Because Your Body Is a Battleground"
	P.O. Box 1830
	Newport, KY 41071-1830

Hold Your Place
Bookmark

You'll always know where you stopped reading with this amazing **wild animal bookmark**. This 4½" to 5" plastic bookmark is colorful and durable and will clasp firmly to your page. The supplier will select one bookmark from an assortment of exotic designs including a tiger, zebra, elephant, giraffe, and parrot. This bookmark will make a great addition to class storytime!

Send:	$2.00 P&H
Ask For:	Wild Animal Bookmark
Mail To:	The Blue Sky Co.
	10877 San Gabriel Way
	Valley Center, CA 92082

A Hypothesis for Having Fun
....
Science Magazine

Science doesn't have to be intimidating. Promote hands-on learning with a **FREE issue of *TOPS Science Magazine***. Kids can learn about oxidation, magnetism, electricity, probability, and more through simple, step-by-step scientific experiments. This 16-page magazine includes several user-friendly illustrations that make learning about science a blast!

Send: $1.00 P&H

Ask For: FREE Issue of *TOPS Science Magazine*

Mail To: TOPS Learning Systems, Dept. 1
10970 S. Mulino Rd.
Canby, OR 97013-9747

The Eyes Have It
....
Vision Program

Every teacher should have a VISION—the **FREE "VISION School Program Guide."** Developed for grades 4–8, this unique science program brings important information on the eyes into the classroom. The 18-page book contains three lesson plans with reproducible handouts. It's designed to help guest speakers lead students in lively interactive sessions on how the eye works, eye problems, and eye safety.

Phone: 1-800-869-2020

Ask For: "VISION Guide"

Or Send Name & Address To: National Eye Institute School Program
2020 Vision Place
Bethesda, MD 20892-3655

Limit: One per classroom

Wave of Patriotism

Mini American Flag

Whether reciting the Pledge of Allegiance at the start of a school day or saluting the flag during the playing of the national anthem, nothing stirs more pride in an American's heart than the Stars and Stripes. Now you can show that pride in your classroom with a **mini 4" x 6" U.S. flag**. This high-quality plastic-coated flag is mounted on a 9" white staff with a red Saf-T-Ball top.

Send: $1.00 P&H

Ask For: U.S. Flag offer FR98

Mail To: Parker Flags, Dept. 5
5750 Plunkett St.
Hollywood, FL 33023

Stick to Studying

Mini Stickers

Your students will feel like winners when you pass out these **200 colorful awards 'n' trophies mini stickers**. These ½" round stickers come in an assortment of bright designs you can use to praise a student's efforts or achievements. Send for them today and make those studying blues go away!

Send: $1.00 P&H

Ask For: Awards 'n' Trophies Mini Stickers

Mail To: The Very Best
P.O. Box 2838, Dept. TR
Long Beach, CA 90801

What's Your Sign?

Sign Language Kit

There are many ways to say "I love you." Do you know how to say it in sign language? Gallaudet University, the nation's foremost center for information on deafness, is offering a **set of sign language learning materials,** including craft projects that teach the sign for "I love you." The package contains five bookmarks featuring the signing alphabet and a list of children's books that help educate kids on how to interact with hearing-impaired people.

Send: $1.50 P&H

Ask For: I Love You Craft offer (specify class grade level)

Mail To: NICD
FR98
800 Florida Ave. NE
Washington, DC 20002

Crafts

Modeling Clay Crafts

Clay Crafts Brochure

Discover Play Clay crafts! With a few simple ingredients, creating colorful crafts is fun and easy. The **FREE "Play Clay" brochure** gives you the recipe for modeling clay and several creative ideas for making jewelry, picture frames, holiday ornaments, and more great projects your students will enjoy doing.

Send: LSASE
Ask For: "Play Clay" Brochure
Mail To: Play Clay
P.O. Box 7468
Princeton, NJ 08540

Keep Cool, Cowboys

Cooler

When the weather is hot, your students can stay cool under the sun with the **Cowboy Cooler**. With this simple kit, all you need to do is put the nontoxic water crystals into the presewn fabric tube, tie it off at the ends, and soak it in water overnight in the refrigerator. All of the materials are included. The Cowboy Cooler ties around the neck and is reusable.

Send: $2.00 P&H
Ask For: Cowboy Cooler Kit
Mail To: Southwest Savvy
P.O. Box 1361-FB
Apple Valley, CA 92307

Soft Touch

Sample

Craft projects look great with Soft Tints Transparent Blending Colors by Delta. Soft Tints produce an antique look on plaster, resin, and ceramic bisque or porcelain, and can be used to create a watercolor effect on wood, paper, glass, and metal. With the **trial-sized gelpak** of Soft Tints, you will also receive a set of **project sheets** filled with useful tips to help you get started.

Send: $2.00 P&H

Ask For: Soft Tints Sample & Ideas

Mail To: Delta, Dept. FBST
2550 Pellisier Place
Whittier, CA 90601-1505

Penned-Up Creativity

Calligraphy Brochure

Explore the art of calligraphy and add a touch of creativity to classroom displays. This **FREE calligraphy brochure and sample art print** is your introduction to a magnificent art form you can learn. Offered by master calligrapher Ken Brown, the booklet provides an overview with definitions, some basic pen stroke techniques, and a catalog of tools and guides to help you get started.

Send: LSASE

Ask For: Calligraphy Brochure and Sample

Mail To: Ken Brown Studio
P.O. Box FR 22
McKinney, TX 75070

Limit: One per household

A Classwarming Gift

Wreath Kit

Steal a little of the Southwest's sunny charm and warm your classroom with this easy-to-make **Southwest wreath ornament kit**. The kit includes natural and red-colored raffia, feathers, and a grapevine wreath. Just follow the illustrated instructions.

> **Send:** $1.75 P&H
>
> **Ask For:** Southwest Wreath Ornament Kit
>
> **Mail To:** Southwest Savvy
> P.O. Box 1361-FB
> Apple Valley, CA 92307

Make Your Own Beanies

Craft Pattern

Popular beanbag critters have made their way into toy stores and into people's hearts. Now students can make their own beanie toys using this **FREE beanie toy pattern**. Fairfield, maker of Poly-Pellets plastic weighted stuffing material, is offering these easy-to-follow directions for making a pair of 10½" Poly Pee-Wee Cats.

> **Send:** LSASE
>
> **Ask For:** Beanie Toy Poly Pee-Wee Cat Pattern
>
> **Mail To:** Fairfield Processing
> P.O. Box 1130-PCats
> Danbury, CT 06813-1130

Get a Glue
Glue Sample

Now you can do all sorts of classroom crafts without the hassle of ordinary, messy glue. Safe, easy-to-use, nontoxic **Kids Choice Glue** cleans up with water. You get instant holding power without the frustration of runny, tacky glues, the heat from a glue gun, or the toxicity of solvent-based glues. Kids Choice Glue is great for paper, wood, felt, leather, cork, fabric, and more. With this introductory offer, you will receive **six trial pillow packs,** each containing ¼ ounce of glue.

Send: $1.00 P&H
Ask For: Kids Choice Glue
Mail To: Signature Marketing
P.O. Box 427
Wyckoff, NJ 07481

Ideas to Scrap
Supply Catalog

Create a class scrapbook to commemorate the school year. Your students will enjoy compiling the materials and decorating the cover. Make your scrapbook stand out by dressing it up with new and colorful decorations. Order the **StarMaster scrapbook supplies catalog,** and you'll get lots of creative ideas and sticker and stationery offers. With your catalog you'll receive a pair of colorful, acid-free, die-cut shapes that you can paste right into your book for instant impact.

Send: LSASE plus 25¢ P&H
Ask For: Die Cuts & Catalog
Mail To: Detra Tolman, StarMaster
2500 Laurelhill Lane
Fort Worth, TX 76133-8112

That's a Wrap ....
Wrapping Gadget

Do you dread wrapping presents because of the hassle tape and scissors cause? You will never have to go through that again when you order the **3 in 1 Super Wrap Mate**. This wrapping gadget cuts cardboard, fabric, gift wrap, and paper. It also has a tape dispenser with tape and a ruler to help you measure what you are cutting.

Send: $2.00 P&H

Ask For: 3 in 1 Super Wrap Mate

Mail To: Surprise Gift of the Month Club
P.O. Box 1-F
Stony Point, NY 10980

Candle Facts
Information Leaflet

Learn some fun and innovative ways to enhance a setting with candles. This **FREE "Candle Facts" information leaflet** tells you the history of candles and gives you fresh ideas on how and where to use them. It includes everything you need to know about candles, such as the proper ways to store and use candles and how to select the perfect candle for any occasion.

Send: LSASE

Ask For: "Candle Facts"

Mail To: National Candle Association
1200 G St. NW, Ste. 760
Washington, DC 20005

Cuckoo for Kokopelli

Craft Kit

Want to ensure that your classroom will be filled with happiness? Since A.D. 500, Native Americans have depicted Kokopelli—the god of harvests, happiness, joy, and prosperity—in their art. Now you can experience that same joy with the **Kokopelli Kit**. The kit includes jute, pony beads, feathers, floral tape, fusible bonding, two different colored fabric pieces, and step-by-step illustrated instructions for making an 11″ high Kokopelli wall hanging or mobile. All you have to supply is a wire coat hanger and a little glue.

Send: $2.00 P&H for one; $3.50 for two
Ask For: Kokopelli Kit
Mail To: Southwest Savvy
Box 1361-KK
Apple Valley, CA 92307

Flower Power

Wreath Kit

You can add the soft touch of flowers to any room with the **Floral Wreath Kit**. Each kit includes a 5″ paper-twist wreath, satin flowers, and matching ribbon. Simply arrange the materials and glue as desired for your own customized wreath. Attach a small wire loop, and the wreath becomes a fancy wall decoration or year-round gift.

Send: $2.00 P&H
Ask For: Wreath Kit
Mail To: Simply Elegant Designs
2248 Obispo Ave., #206
Signal Hill, CA 90806

At Home

A-Peeling Offer
Peeler

Preparing attractive fruits and vegetables is easy with **Chef Harvey's Swiss Peeler**. The precision cutting blade, crafted in Switzerland, is designed to peel and decorate both fruits and vegetables with little effort. It has a high-impact plastic handle formed especially for hand comfort. The peeler washes clean in seconds and stays sharp for years!

Send: $2.00 P&H for one; $1.50 for each additional
Ask For: Swiss Peeler
Mail To: Jaye Products, Inc., Dept. 21
P.O. Box 10726
Naples, FL 34104

For All of Us
Sample Newsletter

Regardless of how much money you make, it's always smart to spend it wisely. To get on the right track, read this **FREE sample issue of *Common Sense at Home.*** It's a smartly written newsletter packed with money-saving advice, including easy-to-make thrifty recipes, water conservation tips, laundry techniques, and more.

Send: LSASE with two first-class stamps
Ask For: FREE Issue of *Common Sense at Home*
Mail To: CSH
P.O. Box 784
Warsaw, MO 65355
Limit: One per household

Maid of Paper

Booklet

With a busy work schedule, you may need a little help around the house. **"999 Helpful Household Hints"** is the next best thing to having a personal assistant. This handy booklet is full of tips for cooking, cleaning, first aid, beauty, gardening, car care, and more. Here is one of the helpful hints you'll find in this guide: use ice to take gum out of clothing. With so much useful information, this is bound to become the most referenced book in your home.

Send: $1.50 P&H
Ask For: "Helpful Household Hints"
Mail To: 21st Century Group
10 Chestnut St.
Spring Valley, NY 10977

You Auto Read This

Sample Newsletter/ Key Tag Protector

Having reliable transportation is important for today's teacher. *Nutz & Boltz* will show you how to keep your car running smoothly without spending excessively. With this **sample issue of the *Nutz & Boltz* newsletter,** you will get information you can't find anywhere else. Plus, as a bonus, you will receive a **key tag protector**. If you ever lose your keys, whoever finds them can drop them in a mailbox. They will be sent to *Nutz & Boltz* and then forwarded to you at no charge.

Send: $2.00 P&H
Ask For: Issue of *Nutz & Boltz* & Key Tag Protector
Mail To: Nutz & Boltz
P.O. Box 123
Butler, MD 21023

A New Invention
Air Freshener

Now you can enjoy the ride to work in sweet-smelling bliss. Patent-pending **Ventsations Scent Clips** are unique vehicle air fresheners designed to slip onto your car's dash and floor vent fins. Ventsations use your air-conditioning and heating systems to dispense long-lasting fragrances. Send for a four-pack of clips in your choice of one of these fragrances: vanilla, apple spice, tropical citrus, rain forest, strawberry, or clean car.

Send: $2.00 P&H

Ask For: Ventsations Scent Clips (specify fragrance)

Mail To: Dakota Products
P.O. Box 1550
Sioux Falls, SD 57101

A Plug for Safety
Pamphlet

The National Electrical Safety Foundation wants to remind everyone to respect the power of electricity. If you are careless, you can get a shock or start a fire. To better protect yourself and your home, the foundation is offering this **FREE "Home Electrical Safety Check."** This informative illustrated **pamphlet** explains basic electrical terms and dispenses valuable advice on how to maintain a safe electrical environment at home.

Send: LSASE with 55¢ postage affixed

Ask For: "Home Electrical Safety Check"

Mail To: NESF
1300 N. 17th St., Ste. 1847
Rosslyn, VA 22209

Limit: One per household

Homeward Bound

Investment Guide

Buying a home is a big investment. That's why it's important to make educated decisions. **"How to Master a House Hunt"** is a **12-step workbook** for prospective home buyers. Prepared by HouseMaster of America, a professional home inspection company, it provides valuable information you should have before signing any contract. A $15.00 coupon toward a HouseMaster inspection is also included.

Send: $2.00 P&H

Ask For: "How to Master a House Hunt"

Mail To: HouseMaster Homeowner Info Center
House Hunt Workbook
421 W. Union Ave.
Bound Brook, NJ 08805

Safe and Secure

Booklet

Whether you live in a house, townhouse, condominium, or apartment building, some simple security measures can safeguard your home and possessions from burglars. An informative new **FREE booklet** called **"Safe & Secure"** can help you protect your residence effectively and with little expense. The colorful 12-page booklet, developed by the Burglary Prevention Council, provides tips on "Your Home's Design" and "Your Neighborhood" and includes a "Vacation Checklist."

Send: LSASE

Ask For: "Safe & Secure" Booklet

Mail To: Burglary Prevention Council
221 N. LaSalle St., Ste. 3500
Chicago, IL 60601-1520

Fun in the Sun
Suncatcher Ornaments

This offer is sure to bring a little sunshine into your home or classroom! This set of **three** friendly, colorful **Suncatcher Ornaments** comes in either a Christmas or Halloween theme. The suncatchers have suction cups for easy attachment. Just leave these decorative ornaments in the sun for a while and watch them come "alive." In the Halloween set, you'll get a pumpkin, witch, and ghost. In the Christmas set, you'll receive a snowman, angel, and Christmas tree.

Send: $2.00 P&H

Ask For: Christmas or Halloween Suncatchers

Mail To: Suncatcher
P.O. Box 1-F
Stony Point, NY 10980

Super Vine
Plant Seeds

In Hawaii's lush rain forests, the woodrose plant blooms yellow flowers that, when dried, turn into a rich brown color, ideal for dry flower arrangements. In your home this vine makes a hardy, fun houseplant that produces rich green leaves in starlike patterns. Use it as a hanging plant or let it climb up poles, stakes, or over bookcases in your home. Guaranteed to grow, these **Hawaiian woodrose seeds** make an ideal gift.

Send: $1.00 P&H

Ask For: Hawaiian Woodrose Seeds

Mail To: Hawaiian Woodrose
P.O. Box 3498
San Rafael, CA 94912

Seal of Approval
Bag Sealer

The **Easy Sealer** is a mini plastic bag sealer about the size of a stapler. Powered by four AA batteries (not included), its contact plates heat up to seal plastic bags smoothly with a quick slide across the opening. Use it in the kitchen to seal in freshness for food or to prevent items from spilling out inside your suitcase when you're on a trip. This product should be used by adults only.

Send: $2.00 P&H

Ask For: Easy Sealer

Mail To: Jaye Products, Inc.
P.O. Box 10726
Naples, FL 34101

Brush Up on Cleaning
Cleaning Brush

Is cleaning getting hard to handle? This popular **HANDI-BRUSH** from Fuller, the makers of fine home products, is just what you need. It is about 6" long, and its unique plastic handle fits perfectly into your hand. This brush is great for cleaning potatoes or scrubbing extra-tough spots on dishes. If you send for the kitchen brush, you will also receive a **FREE Fuller Brush catalog**. This catalog is full of products for keeping the classroom or house tidy.

Send: $1.00 P&H

Ask For: Kitchen Brush & Catalog

Mail To: Richard L. Davis
2605 N. Beltline Blvd.
Columbia, SC 29204

To the Dogs
Pet Behavior Booklet

To help families keep their puppies well behaved, the makers of Resolve Carpet Cleaner have teamed up with professional dog trainer Shelby Marlo to create a **FREE** instructional **booklet** titled **"Help Make Your Family Pet a Top Dog."** Colorful and easy to read, this eight-page booklet offers expert advice on a variety of topics, including bringing home a puppy, and introducing a family dog to a new baby. It also includes tips from the Resolve experts for cleaning carpet stains that can occur when a canine joins the family. With this brochure you will also receive a coupon for $1.00 off Resolve products.

Send: LSASE
Ask For: "Help Make Your Family Pet a Top Dog"
Mail To: Resolve Petcare Booklet
P.O. Box 6245
Young America, MN 55558-6245

Teatime, Nineties Style
Social Guide

Literary tea parties have emerged as an opportunity to discuss favorite authors and enjoy a cup of tea with friends. Presented by Lipton Soothing Moments Teas, this **FREE Guide to "Literary Tea Parties"** shows you how to plan such a get-together. The six-panel brochure includes tips and recipes for hosting a successful literary tea party.

Send: Your name & address
Ask For: "Literary Tea Parties"
Mail To: Lipton Soothing Moments Literary Tea Parties
P.O. Box 1100
Grand Rapids, MN 55745-1100

Grill Out

Newsletter Subscription

The peak of grilling season is during the summer, but the folks at Weber know that some people enjoy grilling all year. With the help of this **FREE subscription to Weber's *Grill-Out Times* newsletter,** you will be able to perfect your grilling skills long after the summer is over. In this newsletter you will find stories from other grill enthusiasts, recommendations on how to throw a great block party, and fabulous recipes that you can prepare on your grill.

Phone: 1-800-99Weber

Ask For: *Grill-Out Times* newsletter

There's No Place Like Home

Decorating Ideas

Do you need new ideas for bringing simple beauty into your life? Do-it-yourself decorating has never been more popular, and this **FREE brochure, "Make Yourself at Home,"** lends ideas ranging from simple table garnishes to sophisticated centerpieces.

Send: Your name & address on a postcard

Ask For: "Make Yourself at Home"

Mail To: California Table Grape Commission
Attn: Wendy Hagar
P.O. Box 27320
Fresno, CA 93729-7320

For Your Munchkin
· · · · · · · · · · · · · · · · · · · ·
Bottle-Feeding Brochure

For a variety of reasons, new mothers sometimes choose to use bottles to supplement breast-feeding. Munchkin, a company that makes feeding products for babies, has designed the 1 STEP™ Disposable Feeding System that actually works best with breast-feeding! This award-winning system is designed to be the healthiest and most natural alternative to Mom. You will receive a **FREE "must-have" brochure** on how you can effectively supplement breast-feeding, along with valuable coupons for Munchkin products.

Send: LSASE

Ask For: Munchkin Brochure & Coupons

Mail To: Munchkin, Inc.

8257 Woodley Ave.

Van Nuys, CA 91406

Books, Magazines & Newsletters

On the Horizon
Retirement Newsletter

If you are near retirement age or you know someone who is, this newsletter will come in handy. **New Horizons** is a monthly six- to eight-page collection of articles from periodicals pertaining to financial planning, health care, travel, leisure, and other topics geared toward seniors. Send for a **FREE sample issue**.

> **Send:** LSASE
> **Ask For:** Sample Issue of *New Horizons*
> **Mail To:** New Horizons
> 484-B Stow Ave.
> Oakland, CA 94606

Toys & Play
Toy Guide

As a teacher, you know that playtime is really important for children. The American Toy Institute, Inc., has put together a **FREE 24-page guide, "Toys & Play,"** designed to help you provide the best play opportunities for children. It describes how the toy industry and government work together to ensure toy safety and offers important guidelines for toy shopping.

> **Send:** Your name & address
> **Phone:** 1-800-851-9955
> **Ask For:** "Toys & Play"
> **Mail To:** Toy Booklet
> 1115 Broadway, Ste. 400
> New York, NY 10010

Children's Wellness
Health Newsletter

Do you want to know more about children's well-being? In this newsletter you will find medical facts on every aspect of children's health, from allergies to X rays. *Your Child's Wellness Newsletter* is a **FREE** eight-page color quarterly publication that discusses issues with information from 20 of the most prominent pediatric specialists in the country. The column "Ask the Doctor" features the specialists' responses to individuals' concerns.

Send: LSASE

Ask For: *Your Child's Wellness Newsletter*

Mail To: Your Child's Wellness Newsletter
c/o H/K Communications
244 Madison Ave., #9H
New York, NY 10016

Kids and the Law
Legal Guide

What you don't know *can* hurt you, especially if you're a parent of a minor. The state of California now has a way to give parents the information they need with **"Kids and the Law: An A to Z Guide for Parents."** Although geared specifically toward California juvenile laws, the book provides information that is applicable to all states. This book is formatted as a simple, indexed guide to statutes regarding minors and tobacco, graffiti, gangs, driving, curfews, drugs, hate crimes, and more. It's **FREE** and is written in easy-to-understand language. This is a great resource for teachers to have on hand.

Phone: 1-800-445-4LAW (1-800-445-4529)

Ask For: "Kids and the Law: An A to Z Guide for Parents"

Only the Best
Magazine Subscription

Although an infant's nourishment may be the most important thing on parents' minds, a new baby has many other needs that must be addressed. To provide information on these matters, Carnation is introducing **"The Very Best" Magazine,** a **FREE** series of seven publications for parents as they progress through pregnancy and the first year of their baby's life. The publications include articles, recipes, coupons, stories, and advice from Dr. Lillian Beard.

Phone: 1-800-965-1200

Ask For: Subscription to "The Very Best" Magazine

Terrific Toys
Special-Needs Guide

If you are a parent, friend, or teacher of a child with special vision needs, get this **FREE "Guide to Toys for Visually Impaired Children"** before you go shopping. The 75 toys listed in this 22-page, full-color booklet have been selected for inclusion by the American Foundation for the Blind because they are considered both fun and safe. Children with visual impairments, child development specialists, and other experts have contributed to this guide.

Phone: 1-800-232-5463

Ask For: "Guide to Toys for Visually Impaired Children"

Presidential Address

Photo Book

Even if your vacation plans or class field trips don't include a trip to the nation's capital, you can still visit this historic place with the **FREE** *White House Photo Tour Book*. Let the White House come to you in this 32-page full-color book, which takes you on a complete tour from the Oval Office to the Rose Garden. No room is off-limits to you, your family, or your class. (Please allow at least 12 weeks for delivery.)

Send: Your name & address

Ask For: *The White House Photo Tour Book*

Mail To: The White House
Washington, DC 20500

Pages of Laughs

Sample Periodical

If laughter is the best medicine, *The Funny Times* is a miracle cure. Now in its 10th year, every monthly 24-page issue is packed with cartoons and stories that will tickle your funny bone. *The Funny Times* features the best work of many well-known writers and cartoonists, including Dave Barry, Molly Ivins, Lynda Barry, Matt Groening, Nicole Hollander, and many others. Send for a sample copy, and you'll wonder how you ever laughed without it.

Send: $1.00 P&H

Ask For: Sample Issue of *The Funny Times*

Mail To: Funny Times
P.O. Box 18530, Dept. 3AB
Cleveland Heights, OH 44118

Reading or Not ...
Book Reviews

Sometimes it's hard to select a good book. That's why a group of publishers has collaborated to create *Eclectic Book Reviews,* a newsletter that reviews many new books on a wide range of subjects. Send for a **FREE** sample of *EBR*. It will save you time by allowing you to make your book selections in advance.

Send: Your name & address

Ask For: FREE Issue of *Eclectic Book Reviews*

Mail To: LA, Inc., Dept. EBR
R.D. 6, Box 41
Monroe, NY 10950

Something for Free
Magazine Offer

Could you or your students use fun items such as rulers, stickers, pencils, novelty erasers, holiday craft projects, and more? Can you use educational items and informative publications? Then you need *FREEBIES Magazine.* Each issue features approximately 100 useful, informative, fun, and seasonal items that are available for free or for a small postage-and-handling charge.

Send: $2.00 P&H for one sample issue; $4.95 for a one-year, five-issue subscription (regular rate is $8.95)

Ask For: Sample issue of *FREEBIES* or a one-year subscription as indicated above

Mail To: *FREEBIES*/Teacher Offer
1135 Eugenia Place
P.O. Box 5025
Carpinteria, CA 93014

FOOD & DRINK

Born and Red in Texas

Citrus Ideas

Grown in the lush subtropical setting of the Lower Rio Grande Valley, Texas red grapefruit is "sweeter by nature." Available in markets only from October through May, this citrus is the reddest, sweetest grapefruit you'll ever see or taste. **"Fun Ideas with Texas Citrus," a FREE brochure,** gives you lots of serving suggestions and recipes for the delicious Texas red grapefruit.

Send: Your name & address

Ask For: "Fun Ideas with Texas Citrus"

Mail To: TexaSweet Citrus Marketing, Inc.
901 Business Park Drive, Ste. 100
Mission, TX 78572

Sea- and Eat-Worthy Recipes

Seafood Recipes

Dive in and cook fish with ease when you have this **FREE brochure, "Savory Seafood Recipes."** This full-color publication features America's favorite seafood products in 11 delectable recipes. A handy reference chart divides species of fish and shellfish by flavor and texture.

Send: LSASE

Ask For: "Savory Seafood Recipes"

Mail To: NFI
1525 Wilson Blvd., Ste. 500
Arlington, VA 22209

Limit: One per household

Global Chicken
Chicken Recipes

Chicken is a favorite food around the world. Because it blends well with all kinds of seasonings, it is equally delicious served spicy hot or delicately mild. This **FREE brochure, "Chicken International,"** is your passport to trying seven poultry dishes with a variety of accents. Recipes include Calypso Caribe Chicken, French Country Chicken Stew, Chicken Thai Stir-Fry, and Chicken Tostadas. All recipes are healthy and easy to follow.

Send: LSASE
Ask For: "Chicken International"
Mail To: Chicken International (FB)
c/o Delmarva Poultry
R.D. 6, Box 47
Georgetown, DE 19947-9622
Limit: One per household

5:15 and All's Well
Recipe Newsletter

If you're like most folks, five o'clock comes and there isn't enough time to plan a big meal. That's where *The 5:15 Times* comes in. All of the recipes call for only five ingredients and take 15 minutes to whip up. This **FREE four-page recipe newsletter** is presented by the makers of Sonoma Dried Tomatoes. The recipes and tips are provided by top chefs and food experts.

Send: Your name & address
Ask For: *The 5:15 Times*
Mail To: 5:15 Times
4791 Dry Creek Rd.
Healdsburg, CA 95448

Rice to the Occasion

Recipe Booklet

You'll love the time-saving cooking tips in the **USA Rice Council's FREE "Quick Tips" recipe booklet.** There are tips for creating European, Asian, South American, and North American dishes, plus hints on grocery buying and advance preparation to reduce cooking time. None of the recipes requires more than seven ingredients, and each takes less than 12 minutes to prepare.

> **Send:** LSASE
> **Ask For:** "Quick Tips"
> **Mail To:** USA Rice, Dept. QT
> P.O. Box 740121
> Houston, TX 77274

What's the Fig Deal?

Fig Facts

California figs have a nutritional value that is unique among other fresh and dried fruits. In celebration of this tasty fruit, the California Fig Advisory Board is offering **FREE "Fabulous Figs, the Fitness Fruit," a set of two brochures** packed with facts, "figures," and recipes that back up the claim that "figs are nature's most nearly perfect fruit." Also included are handling and storing tips as well as serving and snack suggestions.

> **Send:** LSASE
> **Ask For:** Fabulous Figs Brochures
> **Mail To:** California Fig Advisory Board, Dept. F
> P.O. Box 709
> Fresno, CA 93712

Farm Favorites
Low-Fat Recipes

Worried that low-fat means low-taste? For those of you who want to put the flavor back in your diet, Walden Farms has created a **FREE flyer of recipes** that are tasty *and* low in fat. Best of all, they're quick and easy to prepare. Recipes include salad, stuffing, soup, and main dishes featuring chicken.

> **Send:** LSASE
> **Ask For:** Fat-Free Recipes
> **Mail To:** Walden Farms Recipes
> P.O. Box 1398
> Clifton, NJ 07015

Radish Redo
Radish Recipes

Radishes are not just for salads anymore. The Radish Council is offering a **FREE recipe leaflet, "Rave About Radishes,"** with six new ways to enjoy radishes. Recipes include Turkey Pita Pockets with Radish Confetti and Crunchy Radish-Olive Nachos. Complete nutrition facts and buying tips are also provided.

> **Send:** LSASE
> **Ask For:** "Rave About Radishes"
> **Mail To:** Radish Council—FR
> 49 E. 21st St.
> New York, NY 10010

Myriad Mushrooms
Mushroom Booklet

With their intriguing range of tastes and textures, mushrooms are right at the top of the list of versatile vegetables, as you'll discover with this **FREE booklet, "Savor the Possibilities."** It gives information on all the varieties of fresh mushrooms and includes the best way to purchase, store, and prepare them. Full-color photos showcase 16 mouthwatering recipes.

> **Send:** LSASE
> **Ask For:** "Savor the Possibilities"
> **Mail To:** Mushroom Council
> Savor the Possibilities, Dept. F
> 2200-B Douglas Blvd., Ste. 220
> Roseville, CA 95661

Ready for Bread
Bread-Baking Brochure

On a cold winter's day, there's nothing like the wonderful aroma of baking bread. Fleischmann's Yeast and the American Dietetic Association have produced a **FREE brochure** titled **"Rise Up to Good Nutrition,"** full of recipes using a variety of tasty, nutrient-rich ingredients for traditional bread baking and baking with a bread machine, as well as important nutritional information.

> **Send:** LSASE
> **Ask For:** "Rise Up to Good Nutrition"
> **Mail To:** Rise Up to Good Nutrition Brochure
> P.O. Box 7523
> San Francisco, CA 94120-7523

Not Your Ordinary Cheese

Grilled Cheese Ideas

Today's grilled cheese sandwich is no longer limited to just two slices of American cheese on white bread. Mr. Food has teamed up with the American Dairy Association to find the country's most creative and best-tasting grilled cheese sandwiches. The winners are featured in this **FREE "Mr. Food's Grilled Cheese to the Rescue" brochure.** Now you can try some of the country's best grilled cheese sandwich recipes.

Send: LSASE
Ask For: "Mr. Food's Grilled Cheese to the Rescue"
Mail To: American Dairy Association
P.O. Box 760
Rosemont, IL 60018-7760

Cheese, Of Course

Cheese Presentation

A European tradition, the cheese course is now showing up on menus in some of America's most popular restaurants. This **FREE brochure, "The Return of the Cheese Course,"** offers ideas and tips from New York–based restaurateur and entertaining expert Barbara Smith on how to present the perfect cheese course in your own home.

Send: LSASE
Ask For: "The Return of the Cheese Course"
Mail To: American Dairy Association
P.O. Box 760
Rosemont, IL 60018-7760

Cherry-O!

Cherry Recipes

Everyone knows cherries are fabulous in desserts such as pies and cobblers. But you may be surprised to discover this tangy, colorful fruit makes a tasty addition to main courses, side dishes, salads, and beverages. These **FREE "Cherry Delicious Recipes"** introduce you to Party Pasta Salad and Grown-up S'mores. And of course, there's also a recipe for the perfect cherry pie.

Send: Your name & address
Ask For: "Cherry Delicious Recipes"
Mail To: Cherry Marketing, Dept. FB
P.O. Box 30285
Lansing, MI 48909-7785

Not What You Thought

Soy Substitute Samples

It tastes like beef, but it's not. It tastes fattening, but it's not. It tastes like sugar, but it's not. Indulge in the taste of beef, forbidden fattening foods, and sugar with samples of these fantastic soy substitutes. These **samples of Beef Not, Fat Not, and Sugar Not** offer a new way to stay healthy *and* deceive your taste buds. You will also receive a recipe booklet for using soy-based "Not" products in such family favorites as meatloaf and sausage biscuits with gravy.

Send: $2.00 P&H
Ask For: Beef Not, Fat Not, Sugar Not Sampler
Mail To: Dixie Diner's Club
P.O. Box 55549
Houston, TX 77255

Turkey Time
Tasty Turkey Booklet

Today people are turning to turkey for more than just festive holiday meals. It's low in fat, tastes delicious, and is easy to prepare. Plus, as illustrated in this **FREE booklet, "Turkey with a Twist,"** menus can be as varied as the appetites you're satisfying. Presented by Honeysuckle White, this booklet contains 32 traditional to trendy recipes with photos of delectable dishes such as Cashew Turkey Stir-Fry and Turkey Breast à l'Orange.

> **Phone:** 1-800-810-6325
>
> **Ask For:** "Turkey with a Twist"

Kneaded in the Kitchen
Bread Machine Recipes

Do you enjoy baking with a bread machine? If so, then you "knead" this **FREE set of bread machine recipes**. Presented by Saco Cultured Buttermilk and Red Star Yeast, the booklet offers 10 fabulous recipes, including Viennese Mocha Nut and Hearty Multi-Grain. All recipes boast of real buttermilk taste and the health benefits of natural homemade bread.

> **Phone:** 1-800-373-7226
>
> **Ask For:** Saco Bread Machine Recipes
>
> **Limit:** One per person

Olive the Above

Olive Ideas Booklet

Nutrition experts agree that the key to a healthy diet is balance with a variety of foods served in moderation. Because olives are low in calories, sodium, and cholesterol, they make a great addition to many everyday meals. **"Off the Shelf"** is a **FREE 15-page booklet** that presents tempting recipes featuring olives and brand-name ingredients available at your local grocery store.

Send: Your name & address
Ask For: "Off the Shelf" Recipes
Mail To: California Olive Industry, Dept. OTS-F
P.O. Box 7796
Fresno, CA 93747

What's Cookin'?

Recipe Brochure

Honey is the perfect ingredient for cooks on the go and is loaded with natural energy. This **FREE brochure** is for cooks who are **"Squeezed for Time."** Here you'll find quick, delicious, low-fat recipes for cooking with honey, nature's sweetener.

Send: LSASE
Ask For: "Squeezed for Time" Brochure
Mail To: National Honey Board, Dept. FRBE
390 Lashley St.
Longmont, CO 80501-6045

Big Game Sticks
....
Snack Sample

If you are a hungry hunter "boared" with the usual snack choices and on the prowl for something different, you'll want to nab a **Buffalo Bob's Big Game Snack Stick**. This 11" snack stick is made with beef and USDA-inspected farm-raised big game: buffalo, elk, wild boar, kangaroo, or alligator (supplier's choice).

Send: $2.00 P&H

Ask For: Big Game Snack

Mail To: Alvin Peters Co., Dept. BBBG-FB

P.O. Box 2400, EPS

Albany, NY 12220-0400

On the Rhodes
....
Bread Recipes

You're on the road to good eating when you bake Rhodes Bake-N-Serv breads. For a "map" to show you the way, get these **FREE "Classic Recipes for Frozen Roll and Bread Dough."** The booklet shows you how to make authentic Chicago-style pizza, chewy soft pretzels, "dough-so-good" bagels, and more.

Phone: 1-800-876-7333

Ask For: "Classic Recipes"

Limit: One per household

My Love Is RedHot

Barbecue Kit

Do you love hot and spicy foods? The makers of Frank's Original RedHot Cayenne Pepper Sauce have put together a **FREE "Stage a Year-Round Barbecue Bash" kit**. The kit includes recipes, barbecue tips, and a 2.5-ounce bottle of Frank's RedHot Sauce to fire things up. Frank's RedHot enhances the flavor of foods with a rich blend of specially grown cayenne peppers, vinegar, garlic, and spices. From New Year's Day on, make it "RedHot" through all the seasons.

Send: Your name & address

Ask For: "Stage a Year-Round Barbecue Bash" Kit

Mail To: Frank's Original RedHot Sauce
P.O. Box 307
Coventry, CT 06238

Limit: One per household

Fast Recipes

Recipe Booklet

The makers of French's French Fried Onions have put together a **FREE booklet** titled **"Recipe News You Can Use."** The 12 recipes—one for every month of the year—are tasty and innovative. Each one can be made in 20 minutes or less and in three or four steps. A money-saving coupon is included for the star ingredient in all these recipes, French's French Fried Onions.

Send: Your name & address

Ask For: "Recipe News You Can Use"

Mail To: French's French Fried Onions
P.O. Box 6853
Young America, MN 55558-6853

Smart Subbing

Chart

Cook healthier versions of your favorite dishes with suggestions on this **FREE 8½" x 5½" chart**. It lists proper amounts of many healthy ingredients to substitute for high-fat or less nutritional ingredients that are standard in many favorite dishes. For example, use spinach in salads instead of iceberg lettuce, because spinach has more nutrients, and substitute applesauce for butter or margarine in baking recipes.

Send: Your name & address
Ask For: "Sensational Ingredient Substitutions"
Mail To: AICR, Dept. SS
P.O. Box 97167
Washington, DC 20090-7167

Waking Up with the Joneses

Recipe Booklet

Award-winning recipes from America's premier bed & breakfast inns come home to you in a new **FREE Jones Dairy Farm recipe booklet**. The 26-page, full-color booklet features the top dishes selected from Jones Dairy Farm's nationally sponsored competition. Also enclosed are more than $3.00 worth of money-saving coupons for an appetizing array of Jones products.

Send: Your name & address
Ask For: Bed & Breakfast Recipes
Mail To: Jones Dairy Bed & Breakfast Recipe Booklet
c/o Jones Dairy Farm
P.O. Box 23848
Milwaukee, WI 53223-9729

Quaker's Best
Recipe Cards

Quaker Oats™ wants to give you a taste of fame and fortune. Send for this **FREE collection of "Quaker Oats Prize-Winning Recipes."** This set of color cards features delicious dishes concocted by past contest winners. Between July and October, you will also receive the official rules for entering the annual contest. There is one grand prize of $10,000, and there are several other prizes in the adult and children categories.

Send: Your name & address

Ask For: "Quaker Oats Prize-Winning Recipes"
(If between July and October, also request the contest rules)

Mail To: Prize-Winning Recipe Cards
P.O. Box 487, Dept. F
Chicago, IL 60690-0487

Another Fine Pickle
Recipe Brochure

Pickles, pickled peppers, and sauerkraut have few calories and zero fat, and they can add zip and zing to many foods. Send for **"The Secret Is . . ." FREE recipe brochure** offering creative, easy, and surprising dishes made with this trio of pickled vegetables. The 10-panel pamphlet shows you how to shake up the taste of everything from meatloaf to stir-fry to fajitas.

Send: LSASE

Ask For: "The Secret Is . . ."

Mail To: The Secret Is, Pickle Packers International
c/o DHM Group
P.O. Box 767-FB
Holmdel, NJ 07733

How Sweet It Is
Vidalia Onion Recipes

The incomparable sweetness, delicate taste, and incredible texture of Vidalia onions has been inspiring chefs to create extraordinary dishes for years. Send for a **FREE recipe leaflet** with dishes from five prominent American chefs. This mouthwatering collection runs the gamut from soup to pizza.

> **Send:** LSASE
> **Ask For:** Vidalia Recipes
> **Mail To:** Vidalia Onion Committee, Dept. FB
> P.O. Box 1609
> Vidalia, GA 30475

The Royal Blueberry
Blueberry Recipe Book

The authors of **"Let Blueberries Reign All Year Round"** proudly proclaim that the blueberry is the king of all berries. The 76-page book is full of recipes that support their claim. Recipes are included for desserts, salads, jams, beverages, and other goodies. Also featured are plenty of cooking tips and a section on microwave recipes.

> **Send:** $2.00 P&H
> **Ask For:** "Let Blueberries Reign"
> **Mail To:** North American Blueberry Council
> 4995 Golden Foothill Pkwy., Ste. 2
> El Dorado Hills, CA 95742

Fresh Fruit Ideas

Chilean Fruits

The geography and climate of Chile is much like that of California. The same fruits that flourish in California during the summer months ripen on Chilean vines and trees during winter and spring. As a result, we can enjoy Chilean fruits all winter long. With this **FREE recipe brochure, "Bold New Ways with Chilean Fruits,"** you will also receive a **"food safety" fact sheet** and information on these different fruits.

Send: LSASE

Ask For: "Bold New Ways with Chilean Fruits" Brochure and Fact Sheets

Mail To: Fresh Fruit Association
P.O. Box 2410
Sausalito, CA 94966

Have a Feast

Brochure

Eating a variety of fruits and vegetables that help protect against cancer and other chronic illnesses is much easier than you think. Use this **FREE brochure** titled **"Feast on Fruits & Vegetables"** as your planning guide for eating more of these nutritious foods. It provides basic information and delicious recipes to boost fruit and vegetable consumption and lower cancer risk.

Send: Your name & address

Ask For: "Feast on Fruits & Vegetables"

Mail To: The American Institute for Cancer Research
Dept. FF
P.O. Box 97167
Washington, DC 20090-7167

Bayou for You
Seasoning Samples

Straight from K-Paul's Louisiana Kitchen come some great new seasoning mixes. With this trial offer, you will receive two ¼-ounce **samples of Chef Paul Prudhomme's Magic Seasoning Blends** (Magic Seasoning Salt and Herbal Pizza & Pasta Magic). You will also receive a mail-order catalog packed with dozens of fabulous food items and 10 popular Chef Paul recipes.

Send: LSASE

Ask For: Two Samples of Magic Blends plus catalog

Mail To: Magic Seasonings Mail Order FR98
P.O. Box 23342
New Orleans, LA 70183-0342

Spice It Up
Spice Sample

For more than a hundred years, people have loved Watkins food products and their wonderful spices. If you're not in touch with a Watkins dealer, the independent representative below would like to introduce you to or reacquaint you with the company's wide array of products with a **FREE spice sample,** a current **catalog,** and a **coupon** for your next purchase. The sample packet will contain the supplier's choice of black pepper, cinnamon, or a soup base mix.

Send: Your name & address plus two loose first-class postage stamps

Ask For: Watkins Spice Sample

Mail To: Richard Davis, Ind. Rep. #50640
2605 N. Beltine Blvd.
Columbia, SC 29204

Curry Up!
....
Spice Sample

Making exotic Indian cuisine is easy with this **trial pack of Easy Blend Spice Mixtures**. The pack contains three ¼-ounce spice mixes: Tandoori Chicken, Vegetable Spice, and Curry. All the preparation and guesswork of blending the right proportion of spices has been eliminated, so you'll have flawless spicing every time. Recipes are included with each packet.

Send: $2.00 P&H
Ask For: Indian Spice Trial Pack
Mail To: Swahaa Spices
Box 529
Lexington, MA 02173

MONEY MATTERS

Tips from Lake Tahoe

Newsletter

Every day hundreds of people part with their cash in the casinos of Lake Tahoe, but you can hold on to more of your money by living frugally. *The Tahoe Tightwad* is a no-frills **newsletter** based on the motto "promoting thrift as a way of achieving goals." Send for a **FREE** eight-page issue. Past articles have included "Lowering Auto Insurance Costs" and "Try It Free."

Send: LSASE

Ask For: FREE Issue of *The Tahoe Tightwad*

Mail To: The Tahoe Tightwad
P.O. Box 18691
South Lake Tahoe, CA 96151

Stalk Your Stocks

Stock Program

When it comes to stock market trading, it pays to know when to buy and when to sell. **StockVue 2.0** from Alpha Microsystems is a **FREE Internet-based system** that automatically retrieves stock quotes, charts, SEC filings, and news from Quote.com. The program is a complete stock market management system that exports data into popular business applications. StockVue users are alerted by fax, E-mail, or pager of changes in specific stock prices and volume. StockVue can be downloaded FREE via the Internet.

Web Address: http://www.stockvue.com

Green Keeper
Sample Issue

Learn how to get more out of every dollar with a **FREE issue of *Keep Your Cash***. This eight-page publication covers all areas of life from housing and travel to weddings and cleaning products. In this treasury of sensible advice, you'll find cost-cutting recipes, inexpensive crafts, and reader tips presented in a fun-to-read format.

> **Send:** LSASE for one issue
> **Ask For:** *Keep Your Cash*
> **Mail To:** Keep Your Cash
> Box 2234
> Holland, MI 49422-2234

Know Your Plastic
Credit Card Information

Choose from the 100 best unsecured VISA and MasterCard credit cards available in this **120-page book** entitled ***The Insider's Guide to Credit Cards***. From the lowest interest rate and no-annual-fee cards to cash rebate and corporate cards, you'll get information on minimum income requirements, grace periods, credit line ranges, late payment fees, and more. Step-by-step instructions on how to best fill out credit card applications and a list of 25 of the best secured credit cards for those with bad, damaged, or no credit history are also included. You can't beat this deal, which is regularly priced at $35.00.

> **Send:** $5.00 P&H
> **Ask For:** *The Insider's Guide to Credit Cards*
> **Mail To:** Todd Publications
> P.O. Box 301
> West Nyack, NY 10994

Dice Advice

Sample Issue

If you're heading to Las Vegas or another gaming city, you won't want to leave without a **FREE sample issue of *The Crapshooter***. It's the only newsletter in the world devoted exclusively to casino craps. Each issue is brimming with playing strategies, casino news, and other related stories and tips. Past articles include "The Basics of Don't Pass Betting," "Surfing the Craps Web," and more.

Send: LSASE with two first-class stamps affixed
Ask For: FREE Issue of *The Crapshooter*
Mail To: Leaf Press
P.O. Box 421440
San Diego, CA 92142

SPORTS

Olympic Pin-sation
Collectible Pin/Newsletter

It's not too late for you or your students to get a souvenir from the 1992 Olympics. Send for a **collectible Olympic pin** featuring Cobi, the sheepdog mascot of the 1992 Summer Games. Or ask for a ½" x ¾" NBC Sports Peacock pin. You will also receive a **FREE issue of _The Bill Nelson Newsletter,_** the only publication dedicated to the hobby of pin collecting.

Send: $2.00 P&H for one pin

Ask For: Cobi pin _or_ NBC Sports Pin and Newsletter (please specify choice)

Mail To: The Bill Nelson Newsletter
P.O. Box 41630
Tucson, AZ 85717

Roller Roo!
Resource Packet

Roller skating is a fun sport that burns calories and improves the cardiovascular system. You can incorporate it into your physical education curriculum with this Roller Skating Resource Packet. It includes fitness info, safety tips, a poster, cards, stickers, and much more!

Send: $2.00 P&H

Ask For: Roller Skating Resource Packet

Mail To: Roller Skating Association
Attn: Accounting
6905 Corporate Drive
Indianapolis, IN 46278

FAN-tastic Freebies

Fan Packages

Most professional sports franchises have **FREE** materials, such as season schedules and ticket information, that they give away to enthusiastic fans. Some teams even offer free fan packages that may contain stickers, photos, fan club information, catalogs, and more. These souvenirs can be a great reward for hardworking students and make colorful additions to the classroom.

To get these items, all you need to do is write to your favorite baseball, basketball, football, hockey, and soccer teams from the following list. Include your name and address and ask for a **"fan package."** Although not all teams require it, you should send an LSASE to help speed your request. Be sure to include extra postage when writing to Canada. The post office can tell you the current rates for Canada.

If you want to contact a specific player on your favorite team, address the envelope to his or her attention. Keep in mind that because of the high volume of fan mail each team receives, it may take eight weeks or more for a response.

Web site addresses are also listed for some teams. To get more information on your teams through the Internet, see page 89. Many sports organizations provide links to their teams.

AMERICAN LEAGUE BASEBALL TEAMS

Anaheim Angels
P.O. Box 2000
Anaheim, CA 92803

Baltimore Orioles
333 W. Camden St.
Baltimore, MD 21201
http://www.theorioles.com

Boston Red Sox
Fenway Park
Boston, MA 02215
http://www.redsox.com

Chicago White Sox
333 W. 35th St.
Chicago, IL 60616
http://www.chisox.com

Cleveland Indians
2401 Ontario St.
Cleveland, OH 44115
http://www.indians.com

Detroit Tigers
2121 Trumbull Ave.
Detroit, MI 48216

Kansas City Royals
P.O. Box 419969
Kansas City, MO 64141
http://www.kcroyals.com

Minnesota Twins
34 Kirby Puckett Place
Minneapolis, MN 55415
http://www.wcco.com/
sports/twins

New York Yankees
Yankee Stadium
Bronx, NY 10451
http://www.yankees.com

Oakland Athletics
Oakland Coliseum
Oakland, CA 94621
http://www.
oaklandathletics.com

Seattle Mariners
P.O. Box 4100
Seattle, WA 98104
http://www.mariners.org

Tampa Bay Devil Rays
One Tropicana Drive
St. Petersburg, FL 33705

Texas Rangers
P.O. Box 90111
Arlington, TX 76004
http://www.texasrangers.
com

Toronto Blue Jays
One Blue Jays Way,
Ste. 3200
Toronto, Ontario
Canada M5V 1J1
(Note: First-class mail to Canada requires extra stamps.)
http://www.bluejays.ca/

NATIONAL LEAGUE BASEBALL TEAMS

Arizona Diamondbacks
P.O. Box 2095
Phoenix, AZ 85001
http://www.
azdiamondbacks.com

Atlanta Braves
P.O. Box 4064
Atlanta, GA 30303
http://www.atlantabraves.
com

Chicago Cubs
1060 W. Addison St.
Chicago, IL 60613-4397
http://www.cubs.com

Cincinnati Reds
100 Cinergy Field
Cincinnati, OH 45202
http://www.cincinnatireds.
com

Colorado Rockies
2001 Blake St.
Denver, CO 80205

Florida Marlins
2267 NW 199th St.
Miami, FL 33056
http://www.flamarlins.com

Houston Astros
P.O. Box 288
Houston, TX 77001
http://www.astros.com

Los Angeles Dodgers
1000 Elysian Park Ave.
Los Angeles, CA 90012-1199
http://www.dodgers.com/

Milwaukee Brewers
Milwaukee County Stadium
P.O. Box 3099
Milwaukee, WI 53201-3099
http://www.
milwaukeebrewers.com

Montreal Expos
P.O. Box 500, Station M
Montreal, Quebec
Canada H1V 3P2
*(Note: First-class mail to
Canada requires extra
stamps.)*
http://www.
montrealexpos.com

New York Mets
Shea Stadium
Flushing, NY 11368

Philadelphia Phillies
P.O. Box 7575
Philadelphia, PA 19101
http://www.phillies.com

Pittsburgh Pirates
P.O. Box 7000
Pittsburgh, PA 15212
http://www.pirateball.com

St. Louis Cardinals
250 Stadium Plaza
St. Louis, MO 63102
http://www.stlcardinals.com

San Diego Padres
P.O. Box 2000
San Diego, CA 92112-2000
http://www.padres.org

San Francisco Giants
3Com Park at Candlestick
Point
San Francisco, CA 94124
http://www.sfgiants.com

NATIONAL BASKETBALL ASSOCIATION TEAMS

Atlanta Hawks
One CNN Center
South Tower, Ste. 405
Atlanta, GA 30303

Boston Celtics
151 Merrimac St., 5th Floor
Boston, MA 02114

Charlotte Hornets
100 Hive Drive
Charlotte, NC 28217

Chicago Bulls
United Center
1901 W. Madison St.
Chicago, IL 60612

Cleveland Cavaliers
Gund Arena
One Center Court
Cleveland, OH 44115

Dallas Mavericks
Reunion Arena
777 Sports St.
Dallas, TX 75207

Denver Nuggets
1635 Clay St.
P.O. Box 4658
Denver, CO 80204-0658

Detroit Pistons
The Palace of Auburn Hills
Two Championship Drive
Auburn Hills, MI 48057

Golden State Warriors
1221 Broadway, 20th Floor
Oakland, CA 94612

Houston Rockets
Two Greenway Plaza
Houston, TX 77046

Indiana Pacers
300 E. Market St.
Indianapolis, IN 46204

Los Angeles Clippers
L.A. Sports Arena
3939 S. Figueroa St.
Los Angeles, CA 90037

Los Angeles Lakers
Great Western Forum
3900 W. Manchester Blvd.
Inglewood, CA 90306

Miami Heat
Miami Arena
SunTrust International
Center
One SE Third Ave.,
Ste. 2300
Miami, FL 33131

Milwaukee Bucks
The Bradley Center
1001 N. Fourth St.
Milwaukee, WI 53203-1312

Minnesota Timberwolves
Target Center
600 First Ave. N.
Minneapolis, MN 55403

New Jersey Nets
405 Murray Hill Pkwy.
East Rutherford, NJ 07073

New York Knicks
Madison Square Garden
Two Pennsylvania Plaza
New York, NY 10121

Orlando Magic
Orlando Arena
One Magic Place
Orlando, FL 32801

Philadelphia 76ers
One CoreStates Complex
Philadelphia, PA 19148

Phoenix Suns
American West Arena
201 E. Jefferson
Phoenix, AZ 85004

Portland Trail Blazers
One Center Court, Ste. 200
Portland, OR 97227

Sacramento Kings
One Sports Pkwy.
Sacramento, CA 95834

San Antonio Spurs
100 Montana St.
San Antonio, TX 78203

Seattle Supersonics
490 5th Ave. N.
Seattle, WA 98109

Toronto Raptors
20 Bay St., Ste. 1702
Toronto, Ontario
Canada MSJ 2N8
(Note: First-class mail to Canada requires extra stamps.)

Utah Jazz
Delta Center
301 W. South Temple
Salt Lake City, UT 84101

Vancouver Grizzlies
General Motors Place
800 Griffiths Way
Vancouver, British Columbia
Canada V6B 6G1
(Note: First-class mail to Canada requires extra stamps.)

Washington Bullets
USAir Arena
One Harry S. Truman Drive
Landover, MD 20785

WOMEN'S NATIONAL BASKETBALL ASSOCIATION TEAMS

Charlotte Sting
3308 Oak Lake Blvd., Ste. B
Charlotte, NC 28208

Cleveland Rockers
Gund Arena
One Center Court
Cleveland, OH 44115

Houston Comets
Two Greenway Plaza,
Ste. 400
Houston, TX 77046

Los Angeles Sparks
Great Western Forum
3900 W. Manchester Blvd.
Inglewood, CA 90306

New York Liberty
Two Pennsylvania Plaza
New York, NY 10121

Phoenix Mercury
America West Arena
201 E. Jefferson St.
Phoenix, AZ 85004

Sacramento Monarchs
ARCO Arena
One Sports Pkwy.
Sacramento, CA 95834

Utah Starzz
Delta Center
301 W. South Temple
Salt Lake City, UT 84101

AMERICAN FOOTBALL CONFERENCE TEAMS

Baltimore Ravens
11001 Owings Mills Blvd.
Owings Mills, MD 21117

Buffalo Bills
One Bills Drive
Orchard Park, NY 14127

Cincinnati Bengals
One Bengals Drive
Cincinnati, OH 45204

Denver Broncos
13655 Broncos Pkwy.
Englewood, CO 80112

Indianapolis Colts
7001 W. 56th St.
Indianapolis, IN 46254

Jacksonville Jaguars
One Stadium Place
Jacksonville, FL 32202

Kansas City Chiefs
One Arrowhead Drive
Kansas City, MO 64129

Miami Dolphins
7500 SW 30th St.
Davie, FL 33314

New England Patriots
Foxboro Stadium
60 Washington St.
Foxboro, MA 02035

New York Jets
1000 Fulton Ave.
Hempstead, NY 11550

Oakland Raiders
1220 Harbor Bay Pkwy.
Alameda, CA 94502

Pittsburgh Steelers
Three Rivers Stadium
300 Stadium Circle
Pittsburgh, PA 15212

San Diego Chargers
4020 Murphy Canyon Rd.
San Diego, CA 92123

Seattle Seahawks
11220 NE 53rd St.
Kirkland, WA 98033

Tennessee Oilers
Baptist Sports Park
7640 Hwy. 70 S.
Nashville, TN 37221

NATIONAL FOOTBALL CONFERENCE TEAMS

Chicago Bears
1000 Football Drive
Lake Forest, IL 60045

Dallas Cowboys
One Cowboys Pkwy.
Irving, TX 75063

Detroit Lions
1200 Featherstone Rd.
Pontiac, MI 48342

Arizona Cardinals
8701 S. Hardy Drive
Phoenix, AZ 85284

Green Bay Packers
1265 Lombardi Ave.
Green Bay, WI 54304

Atlanta Falcons
One Falcon Place
Suwanee, GA 30174

Minnesota Vikings
9520 Viking Drive
Eden Prairie, MN 55344

Carolina Panthers
800 S. Mint St.
Charlotte, NC 28202

New Orleans Saints
5800 Airline Hwy.
Metairie, LA 70003

New York Giants
Giants Stadium
East Rutherford, NJ 07073

Philadelphia Eagles
3501 S. Broad St.
Philadelphia, PA 19148

St. Louis Rams
One Rams Way
St. Louis, MO 63045

San Francisco 49ers
4949 Centennial Blvd.
Santa Clara, CA 95054

Tampa Bay Buccaneers
One Buccaneer Place
Tampa, FL 33607

Washington Redskins
21300 Redskin Park Drive
Ashburn, VA 22011

NATIONAL HOCKEY LEAGUE TEAMS

Mighty Ducks of Anaheim
Arrowhead Pond of
Anaheim
2695 Katella Ave.
Anaheim, CA 92803

Boston Bruins
Fleet Center
Boston, MA 02114

Buffalo Sabres
One Seymour H. Knox III
Plaza
Buffalo, NY 14203-3096

Calgary Flames
Canadian Airlines
Saddledome
Box 1540—Station M
Calgary, Alberta
Canada T2P 3B9
*(Note: First-class mail to
Canada requires extra
stamps.)*

Carolina Hurricanes
5000 Aerial Ctr., Ste. 100
Morrisville, NC 27560

Chicago Blackhawks
1901 W. Madison St.
Chicago, IL 60612

Colorado Avalanche
McNichols Sports Arena
1635 Clay St.
Denver, CO 80204

Dallas Stars
211 Cowboys Pkwy.
Irving, TX 75063

Detroit Red Wings
Joe Louis Arena
600 Civic Center Drive
Detroit, MI 48226

Edmonton Oilers
11230-110 St.
Edmonton, Alberta
Canada T5G 3G8
*(Note: First-class mail to
Canada requires extra
stamps.)*

Florida Panthers
100 NE Third Ave.,
10th Floor
Fort Lauderdale, FL 33301

Los Angeles Kings
Great Western Forum
3900 W. Manchester Blvd.
Inglewood, CA 90305

Montreal Canadiens
1260 rue de la Gauchetiere
Ouest
Montreal, Quebec
Canada H3B 5E8
*(Note: First-class mail to
Canada requires extra
stamps.)*

New Jersey Devils
Continental Airlines Arena
50 Rte. 120 N.
East Rutherford, NJ 07073

New York Islanders
Nassau Coliseum
Uniondale, NY 11553

New York Rangers
Madison Square Garden
Two Pennsylvania Plaza,
14th Floor
New York, NY 10121

Ottawa Senators
Corel Center
1000 Palladium Drive
Kanata, Ontario
Canada K2V 1A5
*(Note: First-class mail to
Canada requires extra
stamps.)*

Philadelphia Flyers
CoreStates Center
One CoreStates Complex
Philadelphia, PA 19148

Phoenix Coyotes
One Renaissance Square
2 N. Central, Ste. 1930
Phoenix, AZ 85004

Pittsburgh Penguins
Civic Arena
Gate 9
Pittsburgh, PA 15219

St. Louis Blues
1401 Clark Ave.
St. Louis, MO 63103

San Jose Sharks
San Jose Arena
525 W. Santa Clara St.
San Jose, CA 95113

Tampa Bay Lightning
Ice Palace
401 Channelside Drive
Tampa, FL 33602

Toronto Maple Leafs
Maple Leaf Gardens
60 Carlton St.
Toronto, Ontario
Canada M5B 1L1
(Note: First-class mail to Canada requires extra stamps.)

Vancouver Canucks
General Motors Place
800 Griffiths Way
Vancouver, British Columbia
Canada V6B 6G1
(Note: First-class mail to Canada requires extra stamps.)

Washington Capitals
USAir Arena
Landover, MD 20785

MAJOR LEAGUE SOCCER—WESTERN CONFERENCE

Colorado Rapids
555 17th St., Ste. 3350
Denver, CO 80202
http://www.intermark.
com/rapids

Dallas Burn
2602 McKinney, Ste. 200
Dallas, TX 75204
http://www.burnsoccer.com

Kansas City Wizards
706 Broadway St., Ste. 100
Kansas City, MO 64105-
2300
http://www.kcwizards.com

L.A. Galaxy
1640 S. Sepulveda Blvd.,
Ste. 114
Los Angeles, CA 90025

San Jose Clash
1265 El Camino Real,
2nd Floor
Santa Clara, CA 95050
http://www.clash.com

MAJOR LEAGUE SOCCER—EASTERN CONFERENCE

Columbus Crew
77 E. Nationwide Blvd.
Columbus, OH 43215
http://www.thecrew.com

DC United
13832 Redskin Dr.
Herndon, VA 22071
http://www.dcunited.com

New England Revolution
Foxboro Stadium
60 Washington St., Rte. 1
Foxboro, MA 02035

NY/NJ Metro Stars
One Harmon Plaza,
8th Floor
Secaucus, NJ 07094
http://www.metrostars.com

Tampa Bay Mutiny
1408 N. Westshore Blvd.,
Ste. 1004
Tampa, FL 33607
http://www.
tampabaymutiny.com

Health & Beauty

Get the Skinny
Itch Information

In the summer, you've got insect bites, sunburn, and poison ivy to worry about. In the winter, dryness can make your skin unbearably itchy. The makers of Lanacane are offering **FREE Summer Itch Info (April–September)** or **Dry Skin Info (November–March).** Each publication contains tips for treating the most common skin problems of the season.

Send: LSASE

Ask For: Summer Itch Info or Dry Skin Info

Mail To: Lanacane Itch Information Center
P.O. Box 328-LC
White Plains, NY 10602-0328

Walk Right In
Pantyhose Pamphlet

Throughout fashion history, hosiery has been one of women's most important accessories. **"The Sheer Facts About Pantyhose"** is a **FREE pamphlet** that gives you the information you need about sizing, care, and variety, and even includes tips to make your hosiery last longer. To get a "leg up" on your hosiery needs, order this pamphlet today.

Phone: 1-800-346-7379

Ask For: "The Sheer Facts About Pantyhose"

Pain-Free Advice

Fitness Brochures

The makers of Advil are offering **two FREE fitness brochures** for those wishing to maintain an active lifestyle. You may request "Walking Basics" and/or "Play Pain-Free Golf." Each full-color booklet provides expert advice on how to enjoy your favorite activities with fewer aches. Both contain specific exercise instructions. The golf publication includes a money-saving coupon on your next Advil purchase.

Send: Your name & address
Ask For: "Walking Basics" and/or "Play Pain-Free Golf"
Mail To: Advil Forum on Health Education
1500 Broadway, 25th Floor
New York, NY 10036

Waiting to Exhale?

Breath Fresh Sample

Now you can have fresh breath when you need it, even after eating garlic- and onion-laden foods. Send for a **FREE sample six-pack of Breath Fresh** and breathe easy. This all-natural product comes in easy-to-take gel caps that act directly on your digestive system to eliminate bad breath at its source.

Send: LSASE
Ask For: Breath Fresh Sample Pack
Mail To: 21st Century Group
10 Century St.
White Plains, NY 10977

National Kidney Foundation

Organ Donation Brochure

In an effort to increase public awareness of the need for organ transplants, the National Kidney Foundation is giving away this **FREE brochure** about **"The Organ Donor Program."** It provides important facts and a uniform donor card that you can fill out and carry with you.

Phone: 1-800-622-9010

Ask For: "The Organ Donor Program" Brochure

Child Cold Care

Club Information

As a teacher or parent, you appreciate anything that helps take care of children's health during cold season. Now you can **join the Triaminic Parents Club FREE** by calling Triaminic toll free. Members of the Triaminic Parents Club receive the **FREE** quarterly *Parents Club* **magazine,** which includes informative articles on children's health and safety issues, money-saving offers on child safety videos and products, and a variety of valuable coupons for Triaminic cold care products.

Phone: 1-800-330-9878

Ask: To join the Triaminic Parents Club

Intimate Topic

Lubricant Sample and Brochure

Vaginal dryness is a very personal problem that women often find embarrassing to discuss with their doctor. Now there's a better over-the-counter product called Astroglide that can help alleviate this painful and stressful problem. Try this **FREE 5-milliliter resealable tube of Astroglide.** Astroglide is water based, water soluble, and designed to mimic the body's natural fluids. Along with your sample, you will also receive a **FREE brochure** titled **"Vaginal Dryness."**

> **Send:** Two loose first-class stamps
> **Ask For:** Astroglide Sample and Brochure
> **Mail To:** Astroglide
> 3121 Scott St.
> Vista, CA 92083

Creative Hairdos

Hairstyling Device

Put a new twist on that old ponytail with the **Pony Tailor**. Creative hair weaving is easy with this hairstyling device, which features an adjustable loop for better manageability. It is ultraflexible and guaranteed not to break. You will also receive step-by-step instructions for knot and double inversion styles.

> **Send:** $1.00 P&H for one; $2.00 for three
> **Ask For:** Pony Tailor
> **Mail To:** Jingles International
> 301 Spring Creek Drive
> Divide, CO 80814

Mental Illness Facts
Pamphlet Series

In an effort to educate the community at large and reach out to those who need help, the American Psychiatric Association is offering a **FREE 18-pamphlet series** called **"Let's Talk Facts About Mental Illness."** These pamphlets provide current, easy-to-read information on a wide range of topics, including how to cope with AIDS, anxiety disorders, Alzheimer's disease, depression, and substance abuse.

> **Send:** Your name & address
> **Ask For:** "Let's Talk Facts" Series
> **Mail To:** American Psychiatric Association
> Public Affairs, Dept. SFN-1
> 1400 K St. NW
> Washington, DC 20005
> **Limit:** One series of pamphlets

Floss Easy
Flossing Device

Flossing is one of the best things you can do to maintain your dental health. But many people don't floss because it's tedious and unpleasant. **Floss rings** are designed to eliminate the hassle of daily flossing. Just attach some floss to the floss rings, slip the rings onto your fingers, and floss away. It's easy!

> **Send:** $2.00 P&H for one pair
> **Ask For:** Floss Rings
> **Mail To:** Dix Preventative Products, Inc.
> 145 E. 15th St., Ste. 2-A
> New York, NY 10003

Glaucoma Alert
Referral Helpline

Glaucoma, the "sneak thief of sight," is a blinding disease that often shows no symptoms until permanent damage is done. The American Academy of Ophthalmology has an information and **referral helpline** to help you determine if you are at an increased risk. If you are, the academy can refer you to a local ophthalmologist for a **glaucoma exam**. For those with no insurance, this exam is **FREE**.

Phone: 1-800-391-EYES
Ask For: Glaucoma 2001

Professional Look
Hair Care Samples

Jingles™ products, usually available only through professional salons, are designed for optimum performance. They are environmentally friendly, 100 percent biodegradable, and manufactured without any animal testing. With this offer, you will receive **five hair care samples:** Pure Styling Gel, Healthy Hair Shampoo, Nourishing Shampoo, Workout Shampoo, and Moisturizing Conditioner. Each sample is ¼ ounce, enough for one or two uses. You will also receive coupons applicable toward future orders.

Send: $2.00 P&H
Ask For: Hair Care Samples
Mail To: Jingles International
301 Spring Creek Drive
Divide, CO 80814

Me and My Shadow

Eye Shadow Compact

Now it's easy to freshen your makeup wherever you go with this **eye shadow compact**. This 2½" x 4" black compact has 12 fashionable eye shadow colors, a double-tip brush, and a mirror. The sturdy plastic case can be stashed conveniently in your purse.

Send: $2.00 P&H

Ask For: Eye Shadow Compact

Mail To: Jaye Products
P.O. Box 61471
Fort Meyers, FL 33906

Well, Now!

Health Guide

In support of the objectives set by the U.S. Department of Health and Human Services for the promotion of national health and prevention of disease, the makers of Promise Spread have created a **FREE Personal Wellness Guide**. This 28-page booklet details specific steps for planning a wellness routine. The guide includes sections on nutrition, physical activity, stress reduction, and preventive care, as well as a chart to help individuals track their progress.

Send: Your name & address

Ask For: Promise 2000 Personal Wellness Guide

Mail To: Promise 2000 Program
Center for Healthy Living
264 Passaic Ave.
Fairfield, NJ 07004-2595

Pantene for Great Hair
Healthy Hair Brochure

Would you like your hair to look and feel healthier? This **FREE brochure, "Pantene Model Secrets for Healthy Hair,"** presents great advice from Pantene models Tatjana Patitz and Mette Jensen. It features daily steps for preventing hair damage, ways to give fine hair some style, a quiz to determine which hair spray is right for you, and tips for creating a polished look, including how to stop hair from frizzing in bad weather.

Send: LSASE

Ask For: "Pantene Model Secrets for Healthy Hair"

Mail To: Pantene Model Secrets
30 E. 60th St., Ste. 1400
New York, NY 10022-1078

Advice from the Heart
Heart Information

Do you know how to keep your heart healthy? There are specific things every one of us can do to maintain a healthy heart. Developed by Imatron, the company that created the UltraFast CT Scanner for early detection of heart disease, and HeartScan nationwide diagnostic heart health centers, **"HeartScan's Top Tips for Heart Healthy Living"** provides useful **FREE** information on how to get on the path to wellness.

Phone: 1-800-469-HEART (1-800-469-4327)

Ask For: HeartScan Tips

Have a Quiet Diet

Beano Sample and Bulletin

Now you can enjoy all the benefits of healthful food choices without suffering from uncomfortable side effects. Beano is a natural dietary supplement that improves the digestibility of "gassy" foods such as broccoli, cabbage, beans, and whole-grain cereals and bread. Thousands of people have already discovered the advantages of Beano. And you can, too—just call the number below to receive a **FREE sample of Beano**. With your request, you will also receive the **FREE *Beano Bulletin***.

Phone: 1-800-257-8650
Ask For: Beano Sample & *Beano Bulletin*

Snacking Smart

Snack Brochure

There are quite a few benefits to snacking, but unless you are "smart snacking," the negative consequences outweigh the benefits. This **FREE brochure, "Sneak Health into Snacks,"** contains ideas for creating nutritious, delicious snacks for adults and children that help lower the risk of cancer. The brochure offers snacking strategies, dietary guidelines, and healthful snack ideas.

Send: LSASE with first-class postage affixed
Ask For: "Sneak Health into Snacks"
Mail To: The American Institute for Cancer Research
Dept. HS
P.O. Box 97167
Washington, DC 20090-7167

Intensive Treatment

Conditioner Sample

The **Intensive Treatment Conditioner** is a rich formula loaded with herbal extracts, organic moisturizers, natural oils, and essential proteins. It will soften and add body and shine to your hair. The conditioner is excellent for permed or color-treated hair and is usually only available through professional salons. This 1-ounce trial-size packet, which is good for two to four uses, comes with a certificate for future purchases of Jingles™ products.

Send: $2.00 P&H

Ask For: Intensive Treatment

Mail To: Jingles International
301 Spring Creek Drive
Divide, CO 80814

Turn That Frown Upside Down

Pamphlets

Everyone wants to have a beautiful, healthy smile. You will receive **two FREE pamphlets: "Facts About Orthodontics"** and **"New Beginnings: A Head Start for Healthy Smiles."** These pamphlets provide information on potential problems and explain when and why orthodontic treatment may be necessary.

Send: Your name & address

Ask For: "Facts about Orthodontics" and "New Beginnings"

Mail To: American Association of Orthodontics
Dept. CM
401 N. Lindbergh Blvd.
St. Louis, MO 63141-7816

Allergy Relief

Sample and Newsletter

If you're one of the 72 million Americans who suffer from allergies, you'll be happy to know that relief is in sight with these **FREE Tavist Allergy Management Tips**. In addition, you will receive a **copy of the *Allergy & Sinus Alert,*** a **newsletter** produced by Tavist in conjunction with the American Lung Association. A **FREE sample package of Tavist-D** and money-saving **coupons** are also included.

Send: Your name & address

Ask For: Tavist Allergy Management Tips

Mail To: Tavist Allergy Management Tips
P.O. Box 1596
West Caldwell, NJ 07007-1596

All in the Family

Fitness Test

Find out how your family's health and fitness rate by taking the American Running and Fitness Association's **"Fitness Is a Family Affair Assessment Quiz"** in this **FREE brochure**. It contains 30 questions that evaluate the strengths and weaknesses of your family's exercise, nutrition, and diet patterns.

Send: LSASE

Ask For: "Fitness Is a Family Affair"

Mail To: ARFA
4405 East West Hwy., Ste. 405
Bethesda, MD 20814

Six Steps to More Energy

Health Brochure

How often have you seen young students whirling around in constant motion and wished you could bottle up a little of that energy for yourself? This **FREE four-page brochure from the Baylor College of Medicine** gives you suggestions on how to boost your energy level. The easy-to-understand brochure describes six simple ways to increase your energy level, feel better about yourself, and fight fatigue. This is one of a series of eight different FREE brochures. Other available topics cover diabetes, blood pressure, accident prevention, women's health, kids and food, back pain, and healthy marriages.

Send: LSASE (one for each topic requested)

Ask For: Brochure (please specify topic)

Mail To: WCFY Brochures
Baylor College of Medicine
Houston, TX 77030

On the Internet

As every teacher knows, computers are an important part of the classroom. Teachers have discovered that computer programs and Internet Web sites not only can serve as great informational resources, but they also bring variation and inspiration into the classroom by encouraging students to investigate areas of interest to them and to solve problems on their own.

The editors at *FREEBIES* understand that navigating the information superhighway is not always easy. This section focuses on sites on the World Wide Web that are user-friendly, educational, and fun to explore.

Legislative Information

U.S. Congress Information

Created "in the spirit of Thomas Jefferson," **THOMAS** is a United States Congressional Library server devoted to providing information about the U.S. Congress. Among other resources, site visitors have access to bills, advisory board reports, and congressional records. They can also read the U.S. Constitution, learn how laws are created, or send E-mail to any senator.

Web Address: http://thomas.loc.gov/

Walk Like an Egyptian

Historical Information

Travel to the ancient world of the Egyptians. Find out how this society used pictures to communicate, and tour the interior passages of the Pyramids at Giza. Learn all about Egyptian civilization when you visit **Pyramids, the Inside Story**.

Web Address: http://www.pbs.org/nova/pyramid

Cyberschool

Educational Information

The **Cyberschool Magazine** site has everything a teacher could want. The links include science, literature, history, and more. In an entire section devoted to teachers, you can get expert advice on teaching students in today's world. The site also highlights historical expeditions, modern arts of today and yesterday, and science ideas to entertain and challenge the mind.

Web Address: http://www.infoshare.ca/csm

Holy Cow!

Science Exploration

The **Exploratorium** Web site has more to offer than you can imagine. One highlight is the Cow's Eye Dissection site, where you can see and hear an actual dissection. The interactive graphics are fun and interesting. You can learn science facts and other bits of information by following different links.

Web Address: http://www.exploratorium.edu

Animalistic

Pet Information

The **Animal Network** is a great resource for information about your pet, whether it's a dog, cat, fish, lizard, horse, or ferret. At this site, you can discover the latest news in pet care, health, and nutrition. You'll also enjoy the community forums, where you can discuss your pet with other animal lovers.

Web Address: http://www.petchannel.com

Forecast Your Day

Weather News

The experts from the **Weather Channel** keep you up to date at weather.com. You can find out the latest forecast for the day, as well as the weekly forecast for your hometown. Type in a city or state to get the highs and lows, humidity, and barometric pressure. This site is helpful for planning school field trips or weekend getaways.

Web Address: http://www.weather.com

Highway Help

Road Information

Getting ready for an outing always requires some advance preparation. It's good to find out if there is any road work that might delay your travel plans. At this **Rand McNally** site you'll find helpful information about highway construction and news about special events to help you assess hotel availability.

Web Address: http://www.randmcnally.com/tools/dot.html

Let's Talk Math
Communications Project

MathMagic is a **telecommunications** project developed in El Paso, Texas. It helps students improve their problem-solving and communications skills. MathMagic posts challenges according to grade level (K–3, 4–6, 7–9, and 10–12). Teams are paired up to engage in a problem-solving dialogue with students across the country. When an agreement has been reached, one solution is posted for every pair. This site teaches students to communicate using modern technology.

Web Address: http://forum.swarthmore.edu/mathmagic

Resources Galore
Educational Resources

Special Education Resources on the Internet (SERI) is a collection of information for those interested in special education. An entire section is devoted to resources for parents and educators. Topics include attention-deficit disorders and hyperactivity and its associated disorders.

Web Address: http://www.hood.edu/seri/serihome.htm

Career Development
Internship Directory

Whether you are preparing for a career, looking for your first job, reentering the workforce, or considering a career change, an internship will provide you with the on-the-job experience needed to get started. If you are interested in working with young people and their families, this **internship database** lists more than 2,000 paying and nonpaying internships in more than 500 nonprofit service organizations nationwide.

Web Address: http://www.nassembly.org

Park It Here

Park Guide

Whether you are going on vacation or organizing a field trip, the **Park Net site** will help you plan your journey. Brought to you by the National Park Service, this site will guide you to a specific park or allow you to search for parks in your area. Historical facts and information on the natural resources in various parks are available right at your fingertips.

Web Address: http://www.nps.gov

Presidential Address

American Government

Learn about the history of the nation's highest elected office when you visit **The American Presidency site**. Search links to view documents, see election results, check out campaign sites, and explore the presidential libraries.

Web Address: http://www.grolier.com/presidents/preshome.html

Supplies for You

School Supplies

The **National Association for the Exchange of Industrial Resources** is a nonprofit group that collects donations of new, top-quality merchandise and distributes them to schools and other nonprofit organizations nationwide. Check out this site for information on how to donate goods or become a member school and receive supplies.

Web Address: http://www.misslink.net/naeir/naeir.htm

Artistic Point of View
Art Information

The **Art Now Gallery Guide** has information on exhibits and shows at museums and galleries around the world. Art lovers and educators can search for information on artists and peruse an international list of art fairs. This is a great site to visit when you need to plan a field trip to a local museum or collect information on artists for a class project.

Web Address: http://www.gallery-guide.com

On-line Bargains
Computer Shareware

Computer programs are updated so frequently that it is often difficult to keep up with all the current versions. With **Shareware.com,** you can copy thousands of business programs, games, picture files, and audio and video clips at no charge. Save money and time by visiting this great Web site.

Web Address: http://www.shareware.com

A Jungle of Books
On-line Bookstore

Shop for new books and get the lowest prices at the **Amazon** Web site. This superstore offers more than a million titles at 10 to 30 percent off list prices. You can order books on-screen and pay for them by credit card. Delivery for most of the books can be expected within three days.

Web Address: http://www.amazon.com

A Virtual Museum

Science Information

Explore the outdoors and learn all about science at the **Field Museum** Web site. The options at this site are endless. You can visit exhibits, learn science facts, and enter the education page. The latter includes a teacher's guide, complete with a sampling of educational activities for teachers and students.

Web Address: http://www.bvis.uic.edu/museum/

Doctor's Advice

Medical Information

Do you know how to set and reach your own health and wellness goals? How can you help your baby-sitter to do a better job? How does your child's growth and development compare to the national average? Answers to these and hundreds of other questions are at your fingertips through a new helpful medical service called **MedAccess On-Line**. This site offers useful information to guide you through any stage of life.

Web Address: http://www.medaccess.com

Well Traveled

Travel Information

CNN's **Travel Guide** site is useful not only for its collection of maps, but also for its links to Web sites providing travel information for whatever city, state, or country you're viewing. The City Guides section is perfect for learning about your destination, whether foreign or domestic.

Web Address: http://www.cnn.com/TRAVEL/CITY.GUIDES/

Sports On-line

Team Information

For you "cybersport fan-atics" who just can't get enough of your favorite sports team, below is a list of several sites to check out. This is the fastest way to send fan mail or get up-to-date information on all your favorite athletes.

(Listed by league type)

- **National Football League**
  http://www.nfl.com
- **National Basketball Association**
  http://www.nba.com
- **Women's National Basketball Association**
  http://www.wnba.com
- **National Hockey League**
  http://www.nhl.com
- **Major League Soccer**
  http://www.mlsnet.com
- **Major League Baseball**
  http://www.majorleaguebaseball.com
- **Minor League Baseball**
  http://www.minorleaguebaseball.com

Odds & Ends

Applications Made Easy

College Applications

Now there is a great tool for students who are just starting the college application process. Send for *Apply! '98,* a **FREE CD-ROM** containing reproductions of actual applications to more than 600 colleges around the country. This innovation will save time and help alleviate the pressure of trying to create the perfect application.

Apply! '98 provides exact duplicates of each school's application and includes instructions and student data forms. It even has an interview function to help students select the right schools for them. *Apply! '98* offers information on courses, campus life, admissions requirements, and more—all self-reported by each college. Enhanced artwork and video clips create a hip, cool look. A **FREE financial aid handbook** produced with Sallie Mae entitled *How to Apply for a Student or Parent Loan: A Step-by-Step Guide for Stafford and PLUS Loans* is also available on the CD-ROM. The ship date for this offer is September 1, 1998.

Send: Postcard request with name & address

Ask For: *Apply! '98* (Good for Windows and Macintosh systems. Limits may apply.)

Mail To: Apply! '98
P.O. Box 8406
New Milford, CT 06776-9848

E-mail: Apply@aol.com

Web Address: http://www.weapply.com

Halo Up There
. . . .
Angel Pin

Keep your guardian angel close to you with this darling **angel lapel pin**. This little gold-tone cherub is ¾" long and has a clutch backing that will keep it attached securely to your clothes.

> **Send:** $1.00 P&H for one; $2.00 for three
> **Ask For:** Angel Pin
> **Mail To:** Jaye Products Inc., Dept. 2
> P.O. Box 10726
> Naples, FL 34101

Writes of Spring
. . . .
Note Cards

When spring is in the air, so are thoughts of romance. These lovely **"Appalachian Wilds" note cards** are the perfect way to communicate your musings to your sweetheart. This attractively packaged stationery consists of five cards printed on heavy stock with coordinating envelopes. Each 4¼" x 5½" card features a different Appalachian wildflower pen-and-ink drawing. Use the cards all year round to bring spring fever into that special someone's life.

> **Send:** $1.50 P&H
> **Ask For:** Spring Note Cards
> **Mail To:** The Wren's Nest
> 6220 Newbert Springs Rd.
> Knoxville, TN 37920

Cross Your Heart
Copper Cross

Want a colorful accessory you can wear any day of the week? You can get a genuine **enameled copper cross** for just the cost of shipping. Enameling is a centuries-old process by which colored glass is fused to metal to create a unique and lasting piece of artwork. This 2″ handcrafted cross comes in one of seven colors (selected by the supplier) on an 18″ gold-tone chain.

> **Send:** $2.50 P&H
> **Ask For:** Enameled Cross
> **Mail To:** Gee Vee Originals
> P.O. Box 786
> Pine Grove, CA 95665

A Passionate Offer
Flower Seeds

The passion flower is a native of South America. This plant produces glossy green leaves and rapid-growing tendrils with exquisite flowers. These **Passion Flower seeds** mature into a lovely houseplant that will actually grow up to 4″ a day!

> **Send:** $1.00 P&H
> **Ask For:** Passion Flower
> **Mail To:** Passion Flower
> P.O. Box 3498
> San Rafael, CA 94912

A Pair of Hearts

Earrings

If you think you can't afford nice jewelry, take heart. In fact, take two! For the price of shipping, you can acquire this pair of **Swarovski crystal heart earrings,** which regularly sell for $8.95 or more. These earrings feature lovely, faceted 10-millimeter Austrian crystal hearts. The sparkling-clear crystals dangle from French hook earwires that come in your choice of either surgical steel or Hamilton gold.

Send: $2.00 P&H per pair

Ask For: Crystal Heart Earrings (specify steel or gold)

Mail To: D & F Crafts
P.O. Box 385
Myersville, MD 21773

Limit: Five pairs per household

The Red, White, and Blue

Inflatable Stars

Add a little patriotic life to your classroom with these **two inflatable vinyl stars**. You'll receive one red and one blue, each decorated with white stars. These inflatables measure 12" from point to point and feature a self-sealing valve that prevents deflating. The stars are perfect for a display during any American celebration or on a history-based bulletin board. (During the summer, these stars make great pool toys!)

Send: $2.00 P&H

Ask For: Inflatable Stars

Mail To: Lightning Enterprises
P.O. Box 16121
West Palm Beach, FL 33416

Pet Sitting Made Easy

Pet Care Guide

More than 60 percent of all the households in the United States have some kind of pet. According to the American Humane Society, pets are happiest when they're at home, surrounded by familiar sights, sounds, and smells. A professional pet caregiver can care for your pet while you are away. Find out more about the benefits of having a pet sitter at home with the **"Why You Should Use a Pet Sitter" guide** prepared by the National Association of Professional Pet Sitters.

Send: $1.00 P&H

Ask For: "Why You Should Use a Pet Sitter"

Mail To: Why You Should Use a Pet Sitter
National Association of Professional Pet Sitters
1200 G St. NW, Ste. 760
Washington, DC 20005

You Say Tomato

Plant Seeds

Get a pack of **tomato tree seeds** and grow your own plant. The tomato plant can be grown indoors or outdoors, potted or planted in the ground. It can grow up to 10 feet tall and produces large, exotic leaves and fragrant flowers that yield beautiful red fruit up to five months a year. Easy-to-follow growing instructions are included along with a "window greenhouse" for quick seed starting.

Send: $1.00 P&H

Ask For: Tomato Tree Seeds

Mail To: Tomato Tree Seeds
P.O. Box 3498
San Rafael, CA 94912

INDEX

FREE FREE FREE

Something for nothing!!! There are hundreds of dollars worth of useful, informative, and fun items in each issue of **FREEBIES** Magazine. Each issue, published five times a year (for over 14 years), features at least 100 **FREE** and almost-free offers. You'll get household information, catalogs, recipes, health advice, kids toys, jewelry, and more—every offer of every issue is yours for **FREE**, or for a small postage-and-handling charge!

Have you purchased a "Free Things" book before—only to find that the items were unavailable? That won't happen with FREEBIES—*all of our offers are authenticated (and verified for accuracy) with the suppliers!*

❏ **YES!** Send me 5 issues for only $4.95.
(Save over $10.00 off the cover price!)

❏ **YES!** I want to save even more. Send me 10 issues
for only $7.95. (Save 70% off the cover price!)

❏ Payment Enclosed, or Charge my ❏ VISA ❏ MasterCard

Card Number _ _ _ _ _ _ _ _ _ _ _ _ _ _ _ _ Exp. Date _____

Name_____

Address_____

City_____ State _____ Zip_____

Daytime Phone #
( ) _____
(in case we have a question about your subscription)

Cardholder's Signature_____

Send to: *FREEBIES* Magazine/Teacher Offer
1135 Eugenia Place, Carpinteria, CA 93014-5025